PHYSICAL
SCIENCE
PROJECTS
★ for kids ★

A PROJECT GUIDE TO

FORCES

AND

MOTION

Colleen Kessler

Mitchell Lane

P.O. Box 196
Hockessin, Delaware 19707
Visit us on the web: www.mitchelllane.com
Comments? email us: mitchelllane@mitchelllane.com

Mitchell Lane

PHYSICAL SCIENCE PROJECTS
☆ for Kids ☆

A Project Guide to:
Chemistry • Electricity and Magnetism
Forces and Motion • Light and Optics
Matter • Sound

Copyright © 2012 by Mitchell Lane Publishers

Printing   1   2   3   4   5   6   7   8   9

Library of Congress
Cataloging-in-Publication Data

Kessler, Colleen.
 A project guide to forces and motion /
Colleen D. Kessler.
   p. cm. — (Physical science projects for
kids)
 Includes bibliographical references and
index.
 ISBN 978-1-58415-965-0 (lib. bd.)
 1. Force and energy—Experiments—Juvenile
literature. 2. Motion—Experiments—Juvenile
literature. 3. Science projects—Juvenile
literature. I. Title.
 QC73.4.K476 2011
 531'.6078—dc22
                                          2011000721

eBook ISBN: 9781612281070

                                          PLB

CONTENTS

Isaac Newton

Introduction

Physics is the study of **matter** and **energy** and how they interact with each other. Physicists study many things, including **forces** and **motion**. Physics applies to objects on Earth and those beyond Earth. Everything moves. When you are lying in your bed at night and things seem still, the particles that make up your body and the things in your room are moving. Your room is in a house that is on the planet Earth. Earth is spinning on its axis. It is orbiting the Sun. Some scientists believe that even the universe itself is moving.

In physics, motion is described as a change in location of an object. Motion is relative to the observer or another fixed object. Usually we consider motion in relation to the ground or Earth. Even though all matter is constantly moving, we talk about motion in relation to what we see. When a ball rolls by our feet, we say it is moving. When it comes to a stop, it has stopped moving in relation to us.

Scientists have known for a long time that objects on Earth and in space move in expected ways. They haven't always understood why. Seventeenth-century English scientist Sir Isaac Newton penned three laws of motion. The **first law of motion** says that an object in motion will stay in motion, at the same speed and in the same direction, or it will stay at rest, unless an outside force acts upon it. Scientists define *force* as a push or a pull. You push a ball forward when you kick it. You pull it toward you when you pick it up. These forces change the **speed** and direction of the ball. Force can be measured by a mathematical formula. The formula, *force = mass x acceleration (f = ma)*, means that

Newton's First Law
Applied to Rocket Liftoff

"Every object persists in its state of rest or uniform motion in a straight line unless it is compelled to change that state by forces impressed on it."

Before firing:

Object in state of rest, airspeed zero.

Engine fired:

Thrust increases from zero.

Weight decreases slightly as fuel burns.

When Thrust is greater than Weight:

Net force (Thrust – Weight) is positive upward.

Rocket accelerates upward

Velocity increases

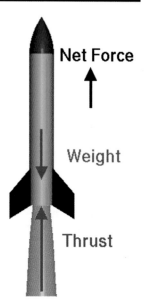

Net Force

Weight

Thrust

the product of the **mass** of an object multiplied by its **acceleration** is the amount of force that was applied.

Newton also discovered a force he called **gravity**. In the story about how he discovered it, an apple falls on his head—but this story is thought to be a myth. More likely, Newton observed an apple falling. He realized that the apple had been still. He knew that some kind of force must have acted upon the apple to pull it down to the ground.

Gravity is so constant in our lives that we barely think about it. You see its effects, though, when you drop a book, jump up (then come down), toss a ball, or get weighed at the doctor's office. Gravity is the pull between two objects. It keeps Earth and all the other bodies in the solar system orbiting around the Sun. It keeps us from flying off into space.

Newton believed that gravity is a force that acts on all matter in the universe. He also stated that it depends on mass and distance. This means that objects with more mass (heavier objects) have more gravitational force than those with less mass. It also means that the force of gravity between objects depends on how close they are. A ball will fall back to Earth when it is tossed up (it is close), yet Mars does not fall into Earth (it is far away).

There are many other kinds of forces, including these:

Centripetal force pulls an object toward the center of a curved path.

Fluid forces such as air pressure or water pressure are exerted by fluid around an object.

Molecular force, such as the pull of a nucleus on an electron, keeps atoms and molecules together.

"Normal" forces are those that act at 90 degrees to a surface.

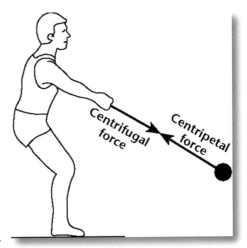

One of them is **centrifugal force**. You feel this when your shoulder pushes on a car door as the car goes around a turn. If it weren't for the door applying this normal force to your shoulder, you would fly out of the car.

In most cases, more than one force is acting on any object at any time. Gravity keeps a motionless soccer ball on the ground, or brings a kicked ball back to the ground. A fluid force—air pressure—presses the skin of the ball outward to keep the ball round. Outside air pressure also pushes on the ball from all around it. When you kick the ball, the force of your kick sends it rolling in the direction of the kick.

Newton's **second law of motion** explains the relationship between force, mass, and acceleration. Mass is the amount of matter something has, and acceleration is change in speed. The harder you kick a soccer ball, the faster it will go. The kick is the force; the mass of the ball stays the same. The acceleration changes according to the force of the kick.

The **third law of motion** states that every action has an equal and opposite reaction. You can't always detect this. When you kick a soccer ball, the same force you apply to the ball is applied to you. The effect of this force is not noticeable because you have more mass than the ball.

Newton's Second Law
Definitions

Differential Form: **Force = change of momentum with change of time**

$$F = \frac{d\,(mv)}{dt}$$

or:

Force = change in <u>mass X velocity</u> with time

$$F = \frac{(m_1 V_1 - m_0 V_0)}{(t_1 - t_0)}$$

With mass constant: **Force = mass X <u>acceleration</u>**

$$F = m\,a$$

Force, acceleration, momentum and velocity are all vector quantities.
Each has both a magnitude and a direction.

Newton's Third Law

Rocket Engine Thrust

Exhaust Flow Pushed Backward

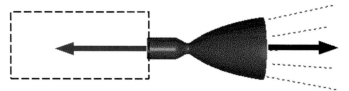

Engine Pushed Forward

For every action, there is an equal and opposite re-action.

When you send a soccer ball down the field, you have done **work**. Physicists define *work* as "force times distance." Although the ball you kicked provides an "equal and opposite reaction" against you, the ball does no work, since it did not move you.

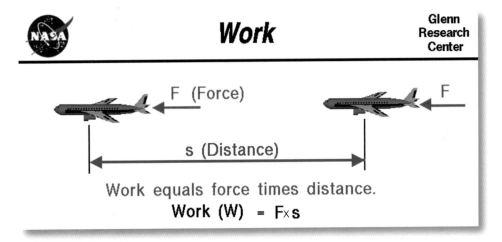

NASA

Work

Glenn Research Center

F (Force)

F

s (Distance)

Work equals force times distance.

Work (W) = F × s

Energy is the capacity to do work. It comes in several forms, including motion, light, heat, and sound. A moving soccer ball gets most of its energy from the person who kicked it. Scientists call the energy in a moving object **kinetic** (active) **energy**.

Just before the ball flies down the field, it has **potential** (stored) **energy**. The air inside the ball pushes against the skin of the ball. When you kick the soccer ball, your foot compresses the air, which momentarily stores the energy. It releases it as kinetic energy when the compressed air pushes back on the dented skin of the ball, and the ball flies through the air.

Energy can be stored and then released (as in a compressed soccer ball), it can be **transferred** to another object (as from your foot to the soccer ball), and it can change forms, but it cannot be destroyed. This is called the **Law of Conservation of Energy**.

Friction is a force that acts in the opposite direction of motion. It occurs whenever two objects touch. The friction between the grooved bottom of your shoes and the rough sidewalk keeps you from slipping as you walk to your friend's house after school. If you tried that same motion on an icy sidewalk, there would be much less friction because of the smooth ice.

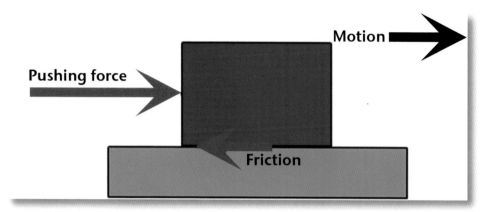

When you are sitting on your bike at the top of a hill, your bike has potential energy. This energy becomes kinetic energy as you coast down the hill. When you tighten the brakes at the bottom, the bike screeches to a stop. The kinetic energy was slowed by the friction of the brakes against the tire rim. The bike's kinetic energy became heat and sound energy as it came squealing to a stop.

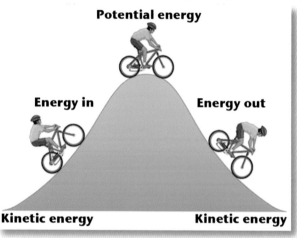

We are surrounded by many different types of forces that result in many different kinds of motion. Energy is transferred and transferred again. In this book, you'll learn more about Newton's three laws of motion and complete an activity or two about each. You will also learn more about friction and gravity. Most important, you'll get a chance to learn firsthand what has interested physicists for centuries.

Read the directions all the way through before you start each experiment, and always work under the supervision of **an adult**. Keep track of your observations in a science notebook. That way you can build on your experiments, and you can go back and check the data you gathered for earlier experiments. As you go, perhaps you'll develop a few theories of your own.

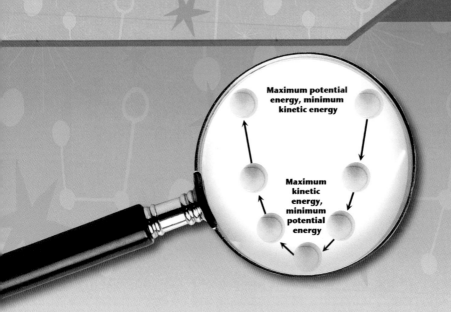

Maximum potential energy, minimum kinetic energy

Maximum kinetic energy, minimum potential energy

BOUNCE A BALL

Suppose you are holding a rubber ball above the ground. How high do you think it will bounce if you drop it to the floor? When things move—like bouncing balls—there is energy change involved.

Anything that moves has kinetic energy. If something is not moving, it has potential energy. The ball you are holding above the ground has potential energy. If you drop it, gravity will pull it down to give it kinetic energy. By letting go, you allow potential energy to change into kinetic energy.

In this activity, you'll observe the change from potential energy to kinetic energy and back. Observe closely, and notice the height of each bounce the ball takes. After you have completed the activity, read the explanation to learn more about energy transfer.

Instructions
1. Hold the ball up high. It has potential energy and no kinetic energy.
2. Let it go. As the ball falls, its energy changes from potential to kinetic. It speeds up as it gains more kinetic energy.
3. Watch the ball hit the floor. When it hits, the kinetic energy is changed again to potential energy—but just for a moment. It

Materials

- Rubber ball or tennis ball
- Hard floor or driveway

bounces right back up again, changing potential energy back into kinetic. How high does it bounce back up? The ball should bounce almost as high as the point where you let it drop.

4. Now, try this again. Let the ball continue to bounce up and down until it stops. What do you notice about each bounce?

Explanation

Each time the ball bounces up, it bounces to a height slightly lower than where it started. It has less potential energy than it started with. How is this possible? In the introduction, you learned that energy cannot be created or destroyed. If this is true, where did the missing energy go?

When the ball hits the ground, friction warms up the rubber. Some of the energy in the ball is changed into heat, or thermal, energy. When the ball bounces a little lower than it started, we know that some of its potential energy changed to thermal energy. None of the energy has been destroyed. It has just changed form.

Inertia Apparatus

AGE-OLD MAGIC

Newton's first law has two parts. The first states that objects will keep moving in the same direction and at the same speed unless a force acts on them. The second part states that an object will stay at rest until a force acts upon it. **Inertia** is the property of resisting a change in motion. All objects have inertia.

This activity demonstrates how friction and inertia can be used to create a magic trick. A bowl of fruit that sits on a table has inertia. Pulling a tablecloth out from under the bowl introduces an outside force. If you pull the tablecloth slowly, there will be plenty of friction between the cloth and the bowl, and the bowl will move, too.

However, if you act quickly enough to overcome the friction between the tablecloth and the bowl, the bowl's inertia will hold it in place. You may want to use a slippery tablecloth to make your job as a magician even easier!

Instructions
1. Place the tablecloth on the table and the bowl of fruit on top.
2. Grab the end of the tablecloth tightly.
3. Pull it as hard and as quickly as you can. The bowl of fruit should stay on the table.

Materials
- Tablecloth
- Table
- Metal or plastic bowl of fruit

Can you use the information that you have learned about Newton's first law to explain why this happens?

Amaze your family and friends with your "magic" trick!

If the bowl doesn't move, you can call yourself a friction magician!

Roller coaster cars are forced through a loop by the track applying a centripetal force on them. The reactive centrifugal force of the cars holds them on the track.

BALL AND STRING

Newton believed that the Moon experiences two forces: gravity and centripetal force. Gravity is constantly pulling the Moon toward Earth. When combined with gravity, the velocity of the Moon's orbit creates centripetal force. (Velocity is speed in one direction, and it is shown as a vector.) In order for the Moon or any satellite to stay in orbit and not fall into its planet, it must have the right combination of gravity, which depends on mass, and centripetal force, which depends on velocity.

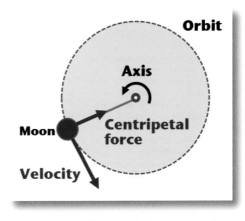

As the Moon orbits, its velocity should cause it to travel in a straight line out into space. Because of the constant gravitational pull between Earth and the Moon, the Moon experiences centripetal force and stays in orbit.

You can observe these forces on a much smaller scale by attaching a string to a ball and swinging the ball in a circle. The ball has momentum, which will carry it around and around. Momentum can be calculated by multiplying an object's mass by its velocity. Centripetal force caused by the string holds the ball in a circular path. If you release

Materials

- **An adult**
- Sharp scissors
- Tennis ball
- Strong string or twine

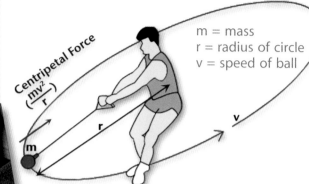

Centripetal Force $\left(\dfrac{mv^2}{r}\right)$

m = mass
r = radius of circle
v = speed of ball

m   r   v

the string, the ball's momentum will carry it along a straight path away from you.

Try this activity outdoors, where there is a lot of space. Use centripetal force to keep a ball moving in a circle. Then release it and see how far its momentum carries it!

Instructions

1. Have **an adult** poke a hole through a tennis ball, thread the string through it, and tie the string securely.
2. Stand in a wide open area and hold on to the string tightly.
3. Swing the ball in a circle over your head as fast as you can.
4. Let go of it.
5. Watch the ball go off in a straight line until gravity pulls it downward.

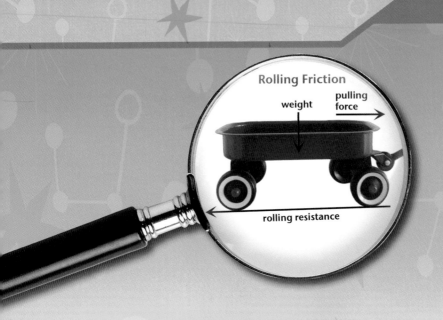

Rolling Friction

weight

pulling force

rolling resistance

RAMPED UP

Newton was able to understand motion because he understood friction. More important, he understood what motion would be like without friction. He knew, though, that friction is always affecting motion.

Friction is always there when an object moves over another object. Have you ever noticed that it feels different to walk across differently textured surfaces? This is because friction is a force that changes based on the surfaces of the things that rub together. This is why it is easier to walk on carpet than on polished wood—the carpet provides more friction.

This activity will help you determine how friction affects motion. The car will move more easily down some surfaces than others based on the friction created. Which surface do you think will cause the most friction? The least?

Instructions
1. Place the wooden board on a stack of books to create a ramp.
2. Attach the soft half of a Velcro strip to the board.
3. Attach the rough half of a Velcro strip to one side of each textured material. (This will make it possible for you to affix the textures to your ramp securely as you test each one.)

Materials

- Wooden board
- Stack of books
- Velcro strips
- Several different pieces of different textured materials (carpet, linoleum, various fabrics, plastic, etc.)
- Toy car or truck
- Stopwatch
- Friend
- Paper and pencil

You can use Velcro dots or strips to hold the materials in place.

TIP: For more accurate results, send the car down each material three times, then average your results for each surface.

Be sure just to let go of the car. You don't want to push it.

4. Give your friend the stopwatch and ask him to time how long the car takes to reach the bottom of the ramp.
5. Attach one of your textures to the ramp.
6. Place the car at the top of the ramp and let go.
7. Record how long it took for the truck to reach the bottom of the ramp.
8. Repeat this activity with each of the different textures, recording the time it took the car to reach the bottom each time.
9. What can you conclude about the effect of different textures on the speed the car is able to travel down the ramp? How can you relate this information to what you know about friction?

CRASH TEST DUMMIES

Newton's second law focuses on the relationship between mass, acceleration, and force. It states that objects will move in the direction of the force that is applied to them. If you push a ball, it will move in the direction that you push.

It also states that the amount of force applied to an object determines the speed of the object. A ball will move slowly if you kick it gently. It will move quickly when you kick it hard.

This law can be applied to people riding in a car. When you travel in a car, the force on your body (F) is the mass of the car you are in (m) times the car's acceleration (a): $F = ma$. Since a car has a lot of mass and moves quickly, its passengers experience a lot of force. What happens to the people inside when the car stops suddenly, as in an accident?

Unless something stops the movement of the people inside, if the car stops suddenly, the people will keep moving. A seat belt connects a person's body to the car, so when the car stops, the person stops, too.

You can observe the relationship between force, mass, and acceleration in this activity. Hopefully, it will also convince you to always wear your seat belt.

Materials

- Doll or action figure
- Toy truck or car
- Large board, slightly wider than your toy car or truck
- A stack of books
- Smooth floor
- Brick
- Rubber bands

Instructions

1. Place one end of a board on a stack of books to form a ramp.
2. Roll your truck or car down the ramp to see how far it goes.
3. Place a brick in the path the truck travels.
4. Put a doll or action figure on the top of the truck and let it go down the ramp again.

Use a doll as a crash test dummy.

No seat belt was used on this run.

5. What happens when the truck hits the brick? What happened to the truck's passenger?
6. Try this again, but this time, secure the doll to the truck with rubber bands.

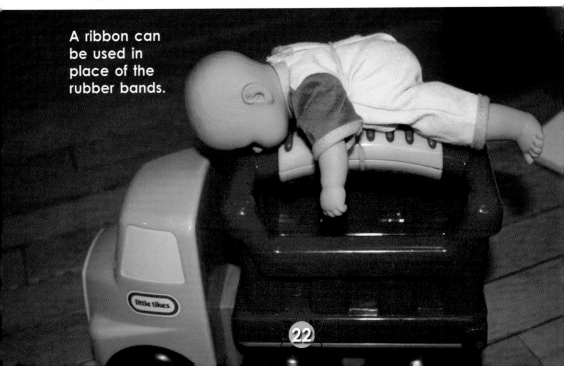

A ribbon can be used in place of the rubber bands.

little tikes

Will the seat belt save the child?

7. What happened this time? Was there a different result? What happened to your passenger this time? Why do you think there are seat belt laws? How does wearing seat belts reduce the number of deaths caused by traffic accidents?

8. Now experiment to see how mass, force, and acceleration relate to one another. Try the experiment again with a heavier doll. What happened? Did the doll's mass make a difference in how far she flew when the truck hit the brick?

9. Try using the original doll, but a heavier or lighter toy vehicle. Now what do you notice? What was the impact like?

10. Finally, try to change the speed of the truck by raising or lowering the ramp. What happened when you made the ramp steeper? Did the truck travel more quickly or slowly? How about when you lowered it? How did the speed affect the crash?

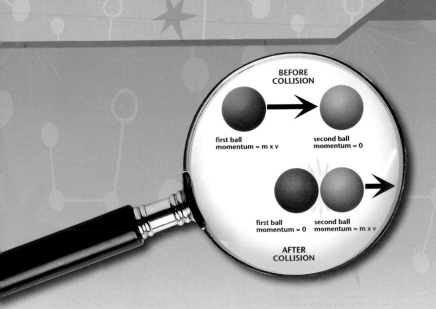

BEFORE
COLLISION

first ball
momentum = m x v

second ball
momentum = 0

first ball
momentum = 0

second ball
momentum = m x v

AFTER
COLLISION

BALL COLLISIONS

Newton's second law ($F = ma$) reminds us that the acceleration of an object depends on the force applied to it.

In this activity you'll experiment with balls that have different masses. The basketball rolling down the ramp will provide force to the balls at the bottom. As long as you release it from the same point on the ramp each time, it will provide the same amount of force each time it hits another ball. Each ball that the basketball hits begins at a speed of zero. Since that is also constant, the only variable, or thing that changes, from trial to trial is the mass of the ball that the basketball hits. Which ball do you think will travel the fastest once it is set in motion by the force of the basketball?

Instructions
1. Using a board and books, make a ramp that faces a wall.
2. Place one ball at the bottom of the ramp.
3. Release the basketball from the top of the ramp so that it hits the ball at the bottom, right at its center.
4. Have your partner start the stopwatch when the basketball starts the motion of the other ball. Have her stop timing when the ball hits the wall.

Materials

- Wooden board
- Stack of books
- Wall
- Basketball
- Several balls of different weights (soccer ball, playground ball, plastic ball, rubber ball, etc.)
- Wooden floor
- Stopwatch
- Partner

Release the ball on the ramp.

Start the stopwatch when the first ball touches the second one.

Try it again with a smaller ball at the bottom.

SAFETY TIP: Keep your shoes on
and tied while doing experiments.

5. Repeat the experiment with each of the other balls.
6. How does the mass of each ball affect its speed when it is hit by
   the basketball?

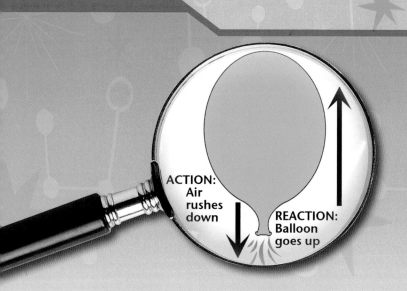

ACTION:
Air
rushes
down

REACTION:
Balloon
goes up

BALLOON BOAT

Newton's third law—for every action there is an equal and opposite reaction—doesn't always seem to make sense.

Think about the last time you blew up a balloon. You may have let go of it before you had a chance to tie it. What happened? The balloon flew away from you and around the room. The air that escaped pushed against the balloon. The balloon pushed away from the air. The air went one way and the balloon went the opposite way. As the balloon pressed the air out through the neck, the air in the rest of the balloon pushed the balloon forward.

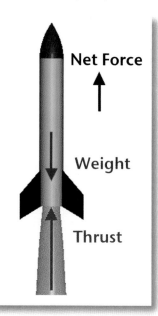

Net Force

Weight

Thrust

This law explains how rockets work, too. The solid fuel that powers a rocket is forced out as a gas through the bottom. The rocket is then pushed in the opposite direction. It goes up. This same reaction pushes your garden hose backward as water is pushed out through the nozzle.

In this activity, you'll use Newton's third law of motion to move a boat through the water in a pool or bathtub.

Materials
- Small plastic container (recycled margarine tub, chip container, yogurt carton, etc.)
- Drinking straw
- Balloon
- Rubber band
- Modeling clay
- Scissors
- Hole punch
- Plastic pool or bathtub filled with water

Instructions

1. Make a hole with your hole punch in the side of your container about ½ inch from the bottom.

2. Using scissors, cut the drinking straw in half.

3. Put one end of the straw into the balloon and wrap the rubber band tightly around it to hold the straw in place.

4. Put the straw through the hole in the container.

5. Secure the straw with modeling clay.

6. Place a ball of clay in the bottom of your container to balance its weight. (Note: You may want to place the boat in the water to achieve the right balance.)

7. Blow the balloon up through the straw and pinch it to keep the air in.
8. Place the boat in the water and release the balloon.
9. What happened? Did your boat go straight? Is there anything you could improve to make it go straighter or faster?

How fast did your boat go?

FARTHER AND FASTER

The force of gravity is constantly and evenly pulling things toward Earth's surface. Gravity will pull all objects toward Earth at the same rate. This means that if you drop two things from the same height, they will hit the ground at the same time. It doesn't matter how much they weigh.

Does this law apply when two things are rolled down a ramp from the same height? In this activity, you'll test your guess. You may be surprised at the results!

Materials
- Two baby food (or similar) jars with lids
- Water
- 2-inch binder

Instructions
1. Fill one jar with water and close the lid tightly.
2. Tighten the lid on the empty jar.
3. Put a binder on a smooth-surfaced floor; the binder will be used as a ramp.

4. Place the jars at the top of the ramp and let them go at the same time.
5. Which jar reached the bottom of the ramp first? Which jar rolled the farthest? Why do you think this happened?

The filled jar reaches the bottom of the ramp first, but the empty jar rolls farther.

The filled jar reaches the bottom first because its mass is distributed more evenly. The empty jar is heavier at its edges. Its mass is not spread

The full jar gets a head start.

The empty jar is on the left.

out evenly. This makes it slower to accelerate than the full jar. As the jars continue to roll, however, the empty jar picks up more speed. When they reach the flat surface, the jar filled with water presses down harder on the floor, creating more friction. Since the empty jar is lighter, it experiences less friction and will continue to pick up speed and roll farther than the full jar.

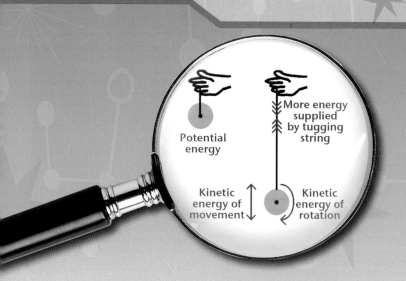

Potential energy

More energy supplied by tugging string

Kinetic energy of movement

Kinetic energy of rotation

PADDLEBOAT

The following experiment puts together many of the physics properties we've learned about so far.

Potential energy is stored energy. You can give a piece of elastic potential energy when you stretch it. That potential energy is transferred into motion when the elastic is released. It is now kinetic energy. This demonstrates the Law of the Conservation of Energy, which states that energy cannot be created or destroyed. It simply changes from one form to another. Potential energy changes to kinetic energy and back again.

When you wind the rubber band on the paddleboat in this activity, you give it potential energy. Releasing the rubber band allows the energy to change from potential to kinetic. When the paddle moves through the water, it obeys Newton's third law of motion. It pushes the water back, and the water pushes the boat forward.

Materials
- Foam board
- Sharp scissors or craft knife
- Rubber band
- Ruler
- **An adult**
- Bathtub or small pool filled with water

Instructions

1. Cut a five-inch-square piece of foam board using sharp scissors. (Or have **an adult** cut it using a craft knife.)
2. Remove a two-inch square from the middle of one side of your foam board square.

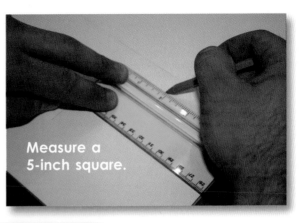

Measure a
5-inch square.

3. Cut a rectangular piece of foam board one inch by two inches. This will be your boat's paddle.
4. If you want to, shape the end opposite of the cut end into a point to form the bow (front) of your boat.

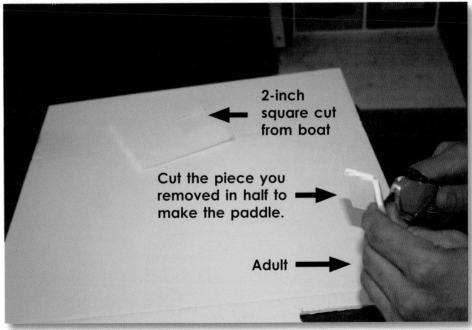

2-inch square cut from boat

Cut the piece you removed in half to make the paddle.

Adult

Wind the rubber band to store potential energy.

5. Stretch the rubber band around the stern (back end) of the boat. The rubber band should stretch across the middle of the square opening.
6. Thread the paddle through the rubber band loop.
7. Spin the paddle to wind the rubber band.
8. Place the boat in the water, holding the paddle still until the boat is in place.
9. Let go of the paddle and boat, and watch the paddle propel the boat through the water.
10. How could you improve your design? What could you do to make your boat go faster?

Watch what happens when potential energy changes to kinetic energy.

ROCKET LAUNCH

All you need to practice rocket science is a little fuel. And you need to know Newton's third law. Pushing fuel down propels a rocket up.

A soda-bottle rocket uses the same physics as the space shuttle or any other rocket. It relies on pressure to force fluid through a small opening at a very high velocity. The force of the fluid being propelled through the opening creates an equal and opposite force that propels the rocket upward.

In a soda-bottle rocket, water is the fluid that propels it up. Compressed air is pumped into it, creating pressure. The air forces the water through the bottle's opening.

As you get ready to launch a soda-bottle rocket, remember that most of the rocket's mass is water. And, with the air crammed inside, it will have a lot of energy. Have **an adult** help you with this

ROCKET PROPULSION

REACTION
Thrust
ACTION
FUEL
Exhaust

FOR EVERY ACTION THERE IS
AN EQUAL AND OPPOSITE REACTION

Oxidizer
(liquid oxygen)

Fuel (liquid)

Pump

Propellant
(a solid
fuel)

Combustion
Chamber

Combustion
Area

Exhaust
Nozzle

Exhaust
Nozzle

LIQUID PROPELLANT
ROCKET

SOLID PROPELLANT
ROCKET

Materials
- **An adult**
- Two-liter plastic soda bottle
- Heavy cardboard or foam board
- Craft blade (for **adult** use only)
- Duct tape
- Rubber cork (available from a science supply catalog, see page 45)
- Hammer
- Nail
- Foot-powered or handheld air pump
- Air valve or needle (used to inflate sports balls)

SODA-BOTTLE ROCKET

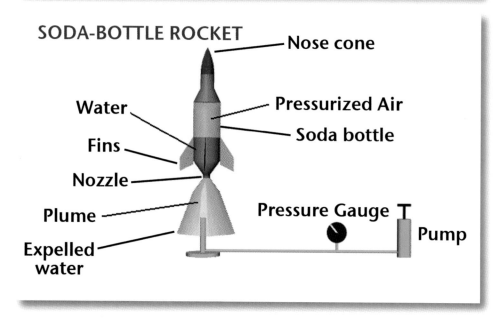

Nose cone

Water

Fins

Nozzle

Plume

Expelled water

Pressurized Air

Soda bottle

Pressure Gauge

Pump

activity. Your rocket could shoot as high as 150 feet (45 meters) or more into the air!

Instructions
1. Rinse the bottle and remove the label.
2. Have **an adult** cut four fins from the cardboard or foam board with a craft knife.

Stand back and watch
the bottle rocket shoot
up into the air.

3. Use duct tape to secure the fins at even intervals on your bottle so that your rocket can stand upright on its own, with the neck facing downward.
4. Have **an adult** use a hammer to pound a nail through the center of a rubber cork, and then remove the nail.
5. Carefully put the valve or inflating needle through the hole made by the nail. (Note: This may be tough because the hole will be tight. Have **an adult** help with this step, too.)
6. Fill the bottle about one-third full of tap water.
7. Shove the cork into the bottle opening. Make sure it is very tight so that no air can escape.
8. Turn the rocket over and stand it up on its fins.
9. Attach an air pump to the valve or needle, then pump air into the bottle. You may notice air bubbles rippling through the water; continue to pump. These bubbles show that pressure is building within the bottle.

10. Once enough pressure has built up, the cork will be forced out of the bottle and it will launch. You'll see Newton's third law in action—the pressure of the air and water pushing downward forces the rocket upward.

Experiment with ways to make the rocket launch higher or straighter. Force the cork in more tightly, add small coins or weights to the nose of the rocket to counterbalance the fins, or add a cone to the nose to make it more **aerodynamic**.

BE SAFE
- **Do this activity in an open, grassy area or on a sports field.**
- **All observers should stand back several meters.**
- **Make sure that your rocket is not pointing toward a person or animal.**

BUILD A BRIDGE

Simple bridges have been around since early times. The first bridges were made by laying trees over streams and rivers. Technology improved, and so did bridge design. Planks of wood and stone slabs were used to make **beam bridges**. Stone slabs support the beam bridge at each end. The planks of wood form a beam that stretches across the stone to span a river, ravine, or other break in solid ground.

Newton's third law of motion can be used to explain how a beam bridge works. The bridge has two main forces. The first is the weight of the bridge itself. The second is the reaction of the bridge's supports. The force of the bridge pushes down, while the equal and opposite reaction of the supports pushes upward. Beam bridges are simple in design, but if too much weight is put on them, they will bend and possibly break.

There are also two other forces at work on bridges: **tension** and **compression**. Compression pushes an object together, making it smaller. Tension acts to pull an object apart. A bridge can buckle when the compression force becomes too strong. It can snap when the

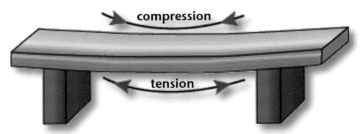

BEAM BRIDGES

Viaduct

Simple span beam bridge

Multiple-span beam bridge

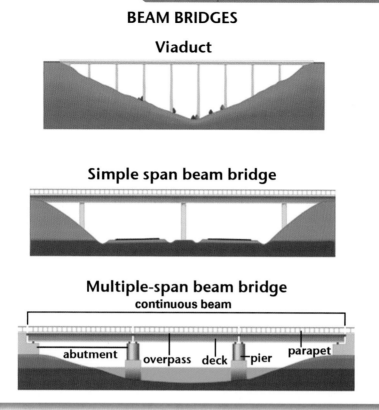

tension gets too strong. When too much weight is put on a beam bridge, the bridge will either buckle due to compression or snap due to tension.

Bridge designers realized that if they spread the forces out, no one spot would receive too much of the force. They needed to spread the force from weaker areas to stronger areas. They began to create beam bridges with arches. The force pushing down on the arch is spread out to the ground.

Arch bridge

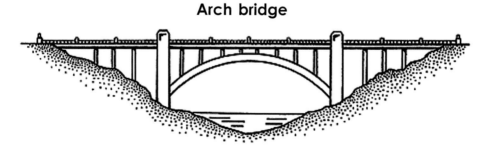

Construct your own beam bridge and see how much weight it can handle.

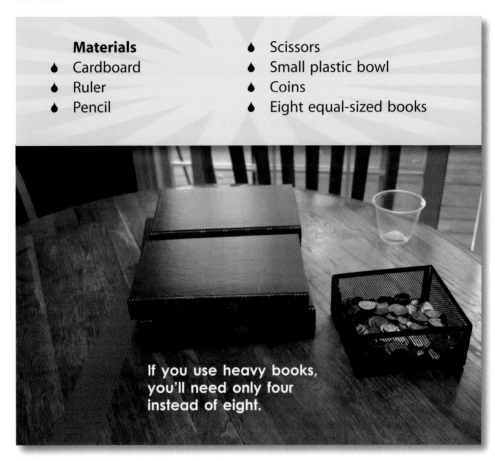

Materials
- Cardboard
- Ruler
- Pencil
- Scissors
- Small plastic bowl
- Coins
- Eight equal-sized books

If you use heavy books, you'll need only four instead of eight.

Instructions
1. Use a pencil and ruler to measure a strip of cardboard 2 feet by 2 inches.
2. Cut out the strip of cardboard with scissors and use the ruler to mark the center point.
3. Pile books in two stacks. Spread them about 10 inches apart.
4. Suspend the cardboard strip between the two columns of books to form a bridge. Secure each side between two books in each stack.
5. Place a plastic bowl on the center point of the bridge.
6. Measure from the tabletop to the top of the bowl with the ruler.
7. Put one coin at a time into the bowl, measuring how much the bridge sags after each addition.

To keep better track of how much weight the bridge holds, use coins that are the same size.

Does adding an arch under the beam make your bridge stronger?

8. Keep adding coins until the bridge touches the tabletop or collapses.
9. Try reinforcing your bridge in different ways. Put a cardboard arch under it, or several tubes. Try different methods of support, measuring the number of coins the bridge can hold before it touches the table or collapses. Which design was most successful?

Books

Bradley, Kimberly Brubaker, and Paul Meisel. *Forces Make Things Move.* New York: HarperCollins, 2005.

Mason, Adrienne, and Claudia Davila. *Move It! Motion, Forces and You.* Toronto: Kids Can Press, 2005.

Sohn, Emily, Steve Erwin, and Charles Barnett. *A Crash Course in Forces and Motion with Max Axiom, Super Scientist.* Mankato, MN: Capstone, 2007.

Welch, Catherine A. *Forces and Motion: A Question and Answer Book.* Mankato, MN: Capstone, 2007.

Works Consulted

Gonick, Larry, and Art Huffman. *The Cartoon Guide to Physics.* New York: CollinsReference, 2005.

Holzner, Steven. *Physics for Dummies.* Hoboken, NJ: Wiley, 2006.

Knapp, Brian J., and David Woodroffe. *Forces.* Danbury, CT: Grolier Educational, 2002.

Kuhn, Karl F. *Basic Physics.* New York: John Wiley & Sons, 1996.

The Nuffield Foundation: Institute of Physics. "Practical Physics." Accessed September 27, 2010. http://www.practicalphysics.org/

On the Internet

BBC School Science Clips
http://www.bbc.co.uk/schools/scienceclips/ages/10_11/forces_action.shtml

Gamequarium Forces and Motions Games
http://www.gamequarium.com/forcesandmotion.html

Science Supply Companies

Science Kit Store
http://sciencekitstore.com/

Science Kit & Boreal Laboratories
http://sciencekit.com/

Steve Spangler Science Store: "Forces and Motion"
http://www.stevespanglerscience.com/category/force-motion

acceleration (ak-sel-er-AY-shun)—Change in speed.

aerodynamic (ayr-oh-dy-NAM-ik)—Streamlined to reduce friction in a fluid.

beam bridge—A simple bridge made up of a horizontal beam(s) supported by vertical posts.

centrifugal (sen-TRIH-fuh-gul) **force**—An apparent force that seems to pull a body outward as it travels in a circular path.

centripetal (sen-TRIH-peh-tul) **force**—The inward pull on a body traveling in a circular path.

compression (kum-PREH-shun)—A force that presses on a body, causing (or trying to cause) it to take up less space.

dense (DENTS)—Having a lot of mass in a unit of volume.

energy (EH-ner-jee)—The ability to do work.

force—A push or a pull.

friction (FRIK-shun)—A force that acts in the opposite direction of motion.

fuel (FYOOL)—A material that provides energy.

gravity (GRAV-ih-tee)—The pull between two objects.

inertia (in-ER-shuh)—An object's resistance to change its motion.

kinetic (kih-NEH-tik) **energy**—Energy of motion.

mass—The amount of matter in an object that gives it weight.

matter—The substance that makes up physical objects.

momentum (moh-MEN-tum)—The property of a moving object that determines how long it will take it to stop; the property depends on its mass and velocity (momentum = mass x velocity).

motion (MOH-shun)—Change in position.

potential (poh-TEN-shul) **energy**—Stored energy.

speed—The measure of distance traveled over a unit of time.

tension (TEN-shun)—A force that pulls on a body, causing (or trying to cause) it to stretch.

transfer—Move from one place to another.

velocity (veh-LAH-sih-tee)—A vector of speed (speed in one direction).

work (WERK)—Force acting over a distance.

Colleen Kessler is the author of numerous science books for Mitchell Lane Publishers, including *A Project Guide to Reptiles and Birds; A Project Guide to Sponges, Worms, and Mollusks; A Project Guide to Electricity and Magnetism; A Project Guide to Sound;* and *A Project Guide to the Solar System;* as well as other books in the Physical Science Projects for Kids series. A former teacher of gifted students, Colleen now satisfies her curiosity as a full-time nonfiction writer. She does her researching and writing in her home office overlooking a wooded backyard in Northeastern Ohio. You can often find her blasting off rockets or searching for salamanders with her husband, Brian, and kids, Trevor, Molly, and Logan, or talking to schoolchildren about the excitement of studying science and nature. For more information about her books and presentations, or to schedule her for a school visit, check out her website at http://www.colleen-kessler.com.